THE CATLINS

AND THE SOUTHERN SCENIC ROUTE

Neville Peat

Otago University Press

Published by Otago University Press
Level 1, 398 Cumberland Street
Dunedin, New Zealand
university.press@otago.ac.nz
www.otago.ac.nz/press

First published 1998
This revised and redesigned edition published 2017.
Copyright © Neville Peat
The moral rights of the author have been asserted.
ISBN 978-1-98-853109-0

Editor: Imogen Coxhead
Index: Imogen Coxhead
Maps: Allan J. Kynaston

Photography by Neville Peat unless otherwise acknowledged.

Front cover: Purakaunui Falls
Back cover: Purakaunui Bay

Printed in China through Asia Pacific Offset.

CONTENTS

ACKNOWLEDGEMENTS

The author is grateful for the information freely given by many Catlins stalwarts over the years. Special thanks to Fergus and Mary Sutherland and Steph Brunton for their advice for this new edition. For the donation of photographs, thanks to Fergus Sutherland, Lou Sanson, Greg Lind, Phil Melgren, Isabella Harrex, Wendy Harrex, Karen Baird, Simon Noble, Nick Smart, Ron Esplin and Yves Kormon.

INFORMATION CENTRES

Visitor information centres in the region are usually open seven days a week in summer. In the quieter months opening hours may be restricted.

- Dunedin i-SITE, The Octagon, Dunedin
- Clutha i-SITE, 4 Clyde Street, Balclutha (located in the community centre on the south side of the Clutha River bridge)
- Catlins Information Centre and Owaka Museum, 10 Campbell Street, Owaka. Email: catlinsinfo@cluthadc.govt.nz
- Waikawa Museum and Information Centre, 604 Niagara–Waikawa Highway, Waikawa
- Fortrose Information Centre (Stirling Tides Café), 5 Moray Terrace, Fortrose
- Invercargill i-SITE, Southland Museum and Art Gallery, 108 Gala Street, Invercargill
- Fiordland National Park Visitor Centre, Lakefront Drive, Te Anau.

WEBSITES

Catlins Coast Inc: www.catlins.org.nz
Clutha District Council: www.cluthanz.com
Venture Southland: www.southernscenicroute.co.nz

THE CATLINS

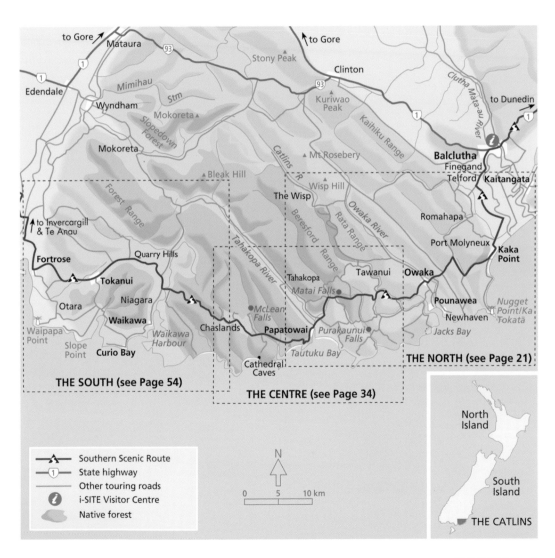

to Gore

Mataura

93

Edendale

1

Stony Peak

to Gore

Clinton

93

to Dunedin

1

Mimihau

Stm

Wyndham

Mokoreta ▲

Slopedown
Forest

Mokoreta

Kuriwao
Peak

Mt Rosebery ▲

Kaihiku Range

Clutha Mata-au River

Balclutha

i

Finegand

Telford

Kaitangata

Bleak Hill ▲

Catlins
R.

Wisp Hill ▲

Forest Range

to Invercargill
& Te Anau

The Wisp

Beresford
Range

Owaka River

Rata Range

Romahapa

Port Molyneux

Kaka
Point

Fortrose

Quarry Hills

Tokanui

Niagara

Otara

Waikawa

Tahakopa River

Tahakopa

Matai Falls

Tawanui

Owaka

Pounawea

Newhaven

Nugget
Point/Ka
Tokatā

McLean
Falls

Waipapa
Point

Slope
Point

Curio Bay

Waikawa
Harbour

Chaslands

Papatowai

Purakaunui
Falls

Jacks Bay

Tautuku Bay

THE NORTH (see Page 21)

Cathedral
Caves

THE SOUTH (see Page 54)

THE CENTRE (see Page 34)

Legend

- Southern Scenic Route
- 1 State highway
- Other touring roads
- i i-SITE Visitor Centre
- Native forest

N

0   5   10 km

North
Island

South
Island

THE CATLINS

1

A NEW FRONTIER

AN ADVENTUROUS and relatively new frontier for tourism, the Catlins coast – known simply as the Catlins – offers visitors something out of the ordinary, something special off the beaten track. Until the 1990s the Catlins projected an image of bush, farmland and wild, lonely coast where few people lived, and the main road running through it had long stretches without tarseal. Its scenic and natural delights were little known outside the south. Today the region keenly welcomes visitors to its piece of 'heartland' New Zealand, and the highway is not only sealed throughout but forms part of the spectacular Southern Scenic Route.

Tucked away in the southeast corner of the South Island, the Catlins imparts a character of its own. You can sense a pioneering spirit in the rough pasture, and catch a glimpse in the bush-clad ridges of the way New Zealand must have appeared before the advent of match, axe, plough and bulldozer. But large-scale clearfelling of native forest is now a thing of the past; people and nature have struck a fairer balance. The Catlins Coastal Rainforest Park is the scenic heart of the region.

There is nothing like the Catlins anywhere else on the eastern seaboard of the South Island. It is a whiff of the West Coast out east – rainforest cloaking coastal hills and ranges, a region not big on towns, or tarseal for that matter apart from the actual highway, with the sometimes wild ocean never far away. The region's northern marker is the coastal township of Kaka Point. From here ridges run inland adjacent to the sprawling flood plains of the Clutha River, New Zealand's largest

LEFT: Nugget Point Light and the razorback section of the walkway.
RIGHT: Waipapa Point Light. YVES KORMON

FOLDS AND FOSSILS

Geologically, the Catlins coast is distinct from the land immediately north of it. Whereas much of Otago is built of a metamorphic rock called schist, the Catlins is mostly made of sedimentary rock: chiefly sandstone, mudstone and siltstone.

The distinction is the work of a geological feature known as the Southland or Murihiku Syncline, where the land has been uplifted, buckled and folded in a particular way. This process, taking millions of years, is manifest in the way the ranges, trending north-west, lie in parallel formation through the region. The youngest rocks are found in the centre of the system. The syncline has been mapped west as far as the Mossburn area in Western Southland.

The rocks are mostly of Jurassic age – 135 to 190 million years old. They were formed by the gradual deposition of sediments, either under the sea or from rivers when the land was above sea level. The sandstone is generally light brown or grey-brown; mudstone is blue-grey and siltstone dark blue. Spasmodically active volcanoes have added ash and other volcanic deposits over the eons.

Because the tectonic pressures in the earth have been relatively gentle, the rocks have retained the fossil remains of numerous Jurassic-age plants and animals. Shellfish are the most common fossils and include brachiopods or lampshells, a filter-feeding shellfish whose ancestry dates back 500 million years, and ammonites, a kind of shell mollusc related to squid and nautilus.

WHY CATLINS?

The Catlins region is named after Captain Edward Cattlin, who bought a large tract of the coast and interior (80km by 64km) from the southern Māori chief, Tuhawaiki, in 1840, a month before the signing of the Treaty of Waitangi. The purchase was later reduced to 100ha by a land court.

Cattlin commanded a schooner that supplied whaling stations in southern New Zealand.

LEFT: Curio Bay.
BELOW: Purakaunui Bay.

river by volume. The southern boundary is Fortrose in Southland, where the hills and wave-pounded bluffs give way to estuaries, wetlands and a clear view west. There are significant and accessible lighthouses at both ends of the Catlins – in the south at Waipapa Point, and in the north at Nugget Point. They are the white bookends of a coastline remarkable for its changing vistas and varied natural features.

The Catlins region also includes ranges and valley floors that stretch inland for up to 40km. Here the land has a distinct 'grain' to it. The main ranges line up roughly parallel, extending inland in a north-west direction. Between them are the main valleys of the Catlins, drained in the north by the Owaka, Catlins, Maclennan and Tahakopa rivers. The smaller Purakaunui, Fleming, Waipati and Waikawa rivers carry less water than the

northern rivers but flow more or less in the same direction. The rivers and streams of the Catlins vary a lot in character – from dark and sluggish to cataracts or crashing waterfalls.

Together the range-and-valley system forms part of the Southland (Murihiku) Syncline (see panel page 8). It is a geological block that causes the main road to run up hill and down dale as it traverses the region. Mt Pye (720m), the highest peak in the Catlins, is set well back from the coast, being 23km from the sea at Tahakopa Bay. Throughout the Catlins coast the ridges meet the sea in dramatic fashion. Just about every coastal landform imaginable is encountered here, thanks to eons of wave action and erosion. Sea cliffs rise an awesome 200m in places, their bases sometimes undercut by caves. Arches and blowholes tell of the collapse of the rock

under assault from the sea. Coves, reefs and rock stacks add rugged decoration to the shoreline. Around any corner, though, the rocky theme can suddenly give way to a picturesque crescent of sand or an estuary gently swept by the tides.

To properly sample this visual drama you will need to explore off the highway – take a side road or two, or walk a coastal track. You do not have to travel very far between attractions; the region is crowded with them.

As with the highway through South Westland, this 'coast road' has little contact with the shoreline; Papatowai and Tautuku Bay offer the closest approaches to the sea from the highway. For much of the way the traveller is passing through old or regenerating forest interspersed with farmland. Some of the farmland has been given over to plantations of pines and other exotic species.

LEFT: Frances Pillars, a group of pointed rock stacks near Tautuku Peninsula. GREG LIND

RIGHT TOP: The estuary and beach at Papatowai.

RIGHT: Tautuku River below McLean Falls.

FIRST FOOTPRINTS

Māori occupation of the Catlins coast goes back some 700 years.

The early people preferred to live by river mouths where they had access to many different kinds of food. Archaeologists who have investigated settlement sites such as those at Papatowai, Pounawea and Cannibal Bay suggest that settlement tended to be in a series of relatively short-term 'waves' rather than a pattern of continuous occupation lasting hundreds of years.

Māori hunted seals and also moa, the large and now extinct flightless birds of New Zealand. By about AD1500 most of the moa had gone, and seals were probably in decline. Māori would have depended then on fish from sea, river and lake, and may have found easier places to live in Otago and Southland where the forest did not present a barrier to overland travel.

The deep forest was a frightening place, for here in the mountains of the Catlins, according to Māori legend, there lived a race of hairy giants known as Maeroero.

It is the native forest that sets the Catlins apart from any other region of the South Island's east coast – cool-temperate rainforest, typically dripping wet, luxuriant, richly textured and reflecting every conceivable shade of green. Logging, sawmilling and farming have made big inroads into the original forest cover in the region's northern and southern zones, but in the central zone the forest predominates. In many places, the bush presses right down to the shoreline and overhangs the cliffs.

Distinctive elements of the forest include the crimson-flowered rātā, prolific tree ferns, scented perching orchids, tall podocarp trees such as rimu, kahikatea and miro, and the smaller pepper tree or horopito, which does especially well where cut-over bush is allowed to regenerate. Hillsides can take on reddish or fleshy hues from the spread of horopito.

BELOW LEFT: Hen-and-chicken fern fronds beside the McLean Falls track. These ferns reproduce from the bulbils or baby fronds that fall off.
BELOW RIGHT: The Catlins' moist climate suits the pepper tree/horopito, which produces red leaves among green ones. **OPPOSITE:** Lichen-encrusted rimu close to the sea on the nature walk to Tautuku Beach.

The protected forest of the Catlins and associated conservation areas cover about 54,000ha, and range discontinuously from the Owaka Valley to the hills west of Waikawa Harbour. In the Chaslands and Tautuku areas, the conservation land links up with coastal native forest that is under Māori ownership, including some that retains podocarp trees of impressive girth and height. Indeed, the biggest podocarps are down by the coast.

Higher up in the central part of the region silver beech forest predominates. Some 6000ha of pure silver beech or tawhai cloak the hills of the hinterland; elsewhere, at lower altitudes, it is mixed with podocarps, rātā and kamahi. Tongues of silver beech are seen on the main valley floors as far south as the Maclennan and Tahakopa valleys, where beech trees are liable to overhang the road. These silver beech forests are the most southerly in New Zealand (beech does not occur on Stewart Island).

Rātā comes into flower spectacularly towards Christmas time, although some years are better than others. Kamahi, also known to southern Māori as towai (hence the name Papatowai, a flat area renowned for its kamahi trees), generally produces its dense creamy flowers between October and December.

OPPOSITE: Crimson rātā blooms colour the reflections at Lake Wilkie.
INSET: Rātā flowers.

WEATHER

Sure, it rains in the Catlins. Without a generous rainfall evenly distributed throughout the year, there would be no rainforest.

Relish the rain and revel in the fine spells. Watch for the magic in the light when the sun emerges after a shower of rain and the green is magnified.

The Catlins climate suffered from bad press early on. The *Clutha Leader* newspaper in 1890 characterised the weather as 'a nasty misty mizzle, a steady dripping drizzle'. The writer overlooked the positives – the relatively mild winters on this coast, and the unlikelihood of snowfalls or extreme cold.

Central and southern areas of the region tend to have more rainfall than the north. Average annual rainfall is 1300mm, spread throughout the year (by comparison, Dunedin receives about 800mm a year). The average number of rain days is impressive – 214. That means you can expect rain almost two days in every three – be it merely a gentle sun-shower or curtains of drenching torrential rain propelled by a vigorous sou-wester. Of course, some of the rain will fall overnight and not affect sightseeing.

Winds from the south-west quarter are most common, with calm weather liable to occur just on half the year. As for temperatures, expect between 10 and 13 degrees Celsius in the mild winter months and 18 to 20 degrees in summer, although temperatures of 30 degrees have occasionally been recorded. A low of minus 7.5 degrees has been recorded at Tautuku.

In this southerly setting, there is an alpine echo in some of the plants. One of them is endemic to the region – the Catlins coastal daisy *Celmisia lindsayii*. It hangs on cliffs from Nugget Point south, a member of the Celmisia group of daisies that are mostly found in the mountains.

CLOCKWISE FROM TOP LEFT: Kamahi in flower in November in Chaslands; The Catlins coastal daisy *Celmisia lindsayii* at Nugget Point; The scented flowers and toothed leaves of New Zealand holly *Olearia ilicifolia*, a tree daisy, on the McLean Falls walkway; Saplings of lancewood and rimu in Lenz Reserve at Tautuku.

Kererū, the New Zealand pigeon.

Among the native fauna there are special elements, too. Long-tailed bats and forest geckos inhabit the bush. There are no kiwi in the region, but the brilliant-coloured yellowhead or mōhua, an endearing forest songbird, is holding on in the face of predation by stoats and rats, thanks to Department of Conservation campaigns. Yellow- and red-crowned parakeets or kākāriki live here. Both species are hole-nesting and rely on old-growth forest for food and nest sites. You may see them in the upper reaches of the Catlins River valley.

There are good numbers of New Zealand pigeon (kererū or kūkupa) in the forested areas, and the migratory shining cuckoo or pīpīwharauroa visits in spring and summer from winter quarters in the Solomon Islands. The South Island fernbird or mātātā, another threatened species, inhabits wetland areas.

Out on the coast the birdlife ranges from the predictable – red-billed and black-backed gulls, for example – to the astounding. In the latter category, watch out for the royal spoonbill (kōtuku-ngutupapa) in estuarine areas – snow-white heron-like birds with black faces and spoon-shaped black bills, which they sweep from side to side through the tidal mud in search

FISHING

The Catlins coast is a haven for anglers. Some come in pursuit of brown trout in the rivers (liberated from 1890), but more try their luck in the briny – either on the estuaries for flounder or along the seashore for blue cod, trumpeter and groper.

Divers target pāua (shellfish in the abalone family) or rock lobster (crayfish), although there are signs at intervals along the coast advising restraint. A few years ago local residents, concerned about the depletion of the pāua beds, instituted a voluntary ban on the commercial harvesting of pāua at several selected sites and a limit of five per day elsewhere in the region for recreational divers.

If you are going fishing in the sea, look for signs that may list restrictions. Marine reserves and other marine protected areas are proposed for the Catlins, Otago and South Canterbury coastal waters following recommendations by the government-appointed Southeast Marine Protection Forum to the minister of conservation and minister for primary industries in 2017.

Male mōhua. PHIL MELGREN

of small invertebrate animals. Small numbers of Australasian gannet (tākapu) fish the inshore seas along this coast.

The feature seabird is the yellow-eyed penguin or hōiho. There are several colonies along the coast, but Roaring Bay near Nugget Point is the best place from which to observe them. Strangely, the Catlins yellow-eyeds prefer to land at rocky sites rather than on soft sandy shores, which is the habit of the Otago Peninsula penguins.

Of special interest to entomologists are the insect communities of the Catlins. As in the region's flora, there are close links with alpine species. Many of the Catlins insects are identical or closely related to alpine or upland species.

The human history of the region is impressively portrayed by two local museums. In 2007 the Owaka Museum, previously housed in cramped conditions, opened in a smart

ABOVE: Surat Bay, a favourite haul-out place for sea lions.

RIGHT: A young elephant seal draped in fronds of bull kelp, Nugget Point. Nowhere common on the mainland New Zealand coast, elephant seals are the world's largest seal species. Adult males can reach 5m in length and weigh 4 tonnes. GREG LIND

The Catlins Information Centre and Owaka Museum Wahi Kahuika occupy this impressive building in Campbell Street, Owaka.

new building with an array of themed exhibits. The Waikawa Museum has also added new exhibits in recent years, utilising a disused school building. Both museums reflect their strong community support. Themes include logging and sawmilling, farming, nineteenth-century lifestyles, Māori history, shipping and shipwrecks, and elements of natural history.

The region still has frontier hallmarks to it. Although farm and forestry developments are less likely these days to encroach on the native forest, the side roads are often narrow and winding, and invariably dressed with gravel rather than tarseal. You can savour remoteness here. One measure of it is the distance between petrol stations (in 2017 no petrol was available between Papatowai and Tokanui, a distance of 53km).

Remoteness brings rewards, too. Over large tracts of the Catlins coast south of Pounawea there is little, if any, pollution of coastal waters by sewage outfalls from human settlements or by industrial discharges, which means that by and large shellfish like pāua are safe to eat.

In a refreshing, energising backblocks region like the Catlins, where the remoteness from city services means you generally have to drive yourself unless you hire a guide, you are entitled to feel like an explorer.

2

THE NORTH

A landmark – the bridge crossing the Clutha River at the entrance to Balclutha.

BALCLUTHA is the regional centre for northern districts of the Catlins and the main town of South Otago. It is on the banks of the Clutha River – Clutha is Gaelic for 'Clyde', the name of a major river in Scotland, and Bal means 'beside'.

From Balclutha the Southern Scenic Route heads south on State Highway 92 through groomed farmland towards the main town of the Catlins, Owaka, 30km from Balclutha. Kaka Point and Nugget Point involve a detour: for southbound traffic the main turnoff is at Otanomomo, 6.5km

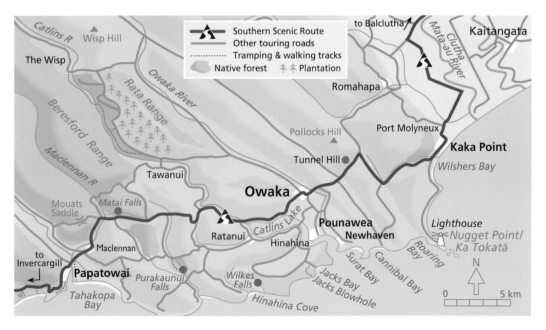

Southern Scenic Route
Other touring roads
Tramping & walking tracks
Native forest · Plantation

Catlins R
Wisp Hill
The Wisp
Rata Range
Owaka River
Beresford Range
Maclennan R
Tawanui
Mouats Saddle
Matai Falls
Maclennan
to Invercargill
Papatowai
Purakaunui Falls
Tahakopa Bay
Ratanui
Catlins Lake
Hinahina
Wilkes Falls
Hinahina Cove
Owaka
Pounawea
Newhaven
Surat Bay
Jacks Bay
Jacks Blowhole
Cannibal Bay
Roaring Bay
Pollocks Hill
Tunnel Hill
Romahapa
Port Molyneux
to Balclutha
Kaitangata
Clutha / Mata-au River
Kaka Point
Wilshers Bay
Lighthouse
Nugget Point/
Ka Tokatā
N
0   5 km

from Balclutha, while northbound traffic can turn off on the north side of Tunnel Hill. At Otanomomo there is a remnant patch of native podocarp forest that stands out in stark contrast to the surrounding farmland.

The road to Kaka Point closes on the coast at a place called Port Molyneux (18km from Balclutha), which is a port in name only. The harbour disappeared when a massive flood in the Clutha River in 1878 forged a new outlet to the north, leaving a sandbank where water once flowed, ships tied up and shops and hotels flourished.

KAKA POINT

Around the corner from Port Molyneux is Kaka Point, a seaside holiday township 21km from Balclutha and 8km from Nugget Point. The town has a general store that acts also as a post office, café and gallery – a versatile store for a versatile township.

Here you can go beachcombing or surfing (the beach is patrolled by lifesavers from November to March), or bushwalking in a superb stand of native forest practically within earshot of the surf.

The bush walk, an easy 30 minutes return, connects the camping ground (cabins, power points and tent spaces) with Totara Street. You won't see the native forest parrot for whom the town is named, but other birds of the bush are plentiful, including bellbirds, fantails, grey warblers, tomtits and pigeons. Rimu and matai trees stand out above the canopy. Note how

Willsher Bay west of Kaka Point village on the road to Nugget Point.

SCANDAL

The Willsher Bay area was stunned by a scandal in the early 1900s. A slightly built young man by the name of Percival Redwood came to stay at the Ottoway family's Nuggets Guest House and soon won the affections of Agnes (Nessie) Ottoway, the 32-year-old daughter. Percy claimed to be the son of a wealthy Hamilton widow and nephew of an archbishop. A sumptuous wedding was arranged. Guests included the local member of parliament. Then came an awful shock: the groom was an imposter – none other than the notorious Miss Amy Maud Bock.

In May 1909 in the Dunedin Supreme Court, Amy Bock pleaded guilty to charges of forgery and false pretences and was sentenced to two years' hard labour. The court declared her a habitual criminal as by this time she had jail sentences totalling 16 years for a series of confidence tricks around the country. Her Nuggets escapade, though, was perhaps her most daring.

TOP: Tirohanga on the road to Nugget Point. **ABOVE**: Settler history: the Willsher Bay memorial cairn salutes the landing in 1840 of a group of European settlers. The smaller plaque below commemorates the 150th anniversary of the visit of surveyor Frederick Tuckett in 1844.

most of the streets are named after native trees.

Kaka Point comes alive in summer when there are events such as a surf carnival, and a bonfire on the beach on 31 December – a popular way for locals and visitors to see in the new year. A local brewery produces a distinctive line of craft beer.

At Willsher Bay, 2km along the road to Nugget Point, there is a stone cairn at the Karoro Road corner dedicated to the first European settlers, a party of four led by George Willsher who landed in June 1840. Willsher was the agent of a Sydney man, Thomas Jones, who had bought land in the district. The settlement failed, however, and Willsher returned to England about 1860. Of the four would-be settlers, only one, Thomas Russell, spent the rest of his life in Otago.

The road to Nugget Point passes Nuggetburn, the site of a shore whaling station and, more recently, an unusual fishing base where, in the absence of a safe mooring, the boats were winched ashore.

An aerial view of Nugget Point. The viewing platform is beside the lighthouse. Roaring Bay is at the upper left. Beyond Campbell Point at right is Willsher Bay. KAREN BAIRD/DOC

NUGGET POINT

Thirty km from Balclutha is Nugget Point (Ka Tokatā), the best-known coastal landmark in the Catlins. The headland, a 47ha scientific reserve under Department of Conservation management, has many natural features not to mention dramatic views. The road to the carpark high on the headland narrows as it leaves the shoreline, so drive carefully. At a saddle before the road-end there is a signposted track to a yellow-eyed penguin hide at Roaring Bay. Binoculars are useful for spotting seals along the shoreline and at the destination, the lighthouse on the point.

The walking track to Nugget Point starts from the carpark and toilets at the road-end. The 900m gently graded walk takes about 15 minutes one way, but be prepared for sudden changes in the weather. The wind-shorn vegetation is a clue to the wind velocities that can occur here. In the dip before you reach the lighthouse and two-deck viewing platform, the track crosses a razorback ridge that offers views on both sides of the headland. By now you will realise you are visiting the edge of somewhere special.

The area takes its name from the wave-eroded rock stacks and islets, which bear some resemblance to gold nuggets. Note their curious vertical stripes. They represent layers of

NUGGETS LIGHT

Nugget Point lighthouse, 9.5m high, stands 76m above sea level. It was built of locally quarried stone in 1869–70. Now automated, the light flashes twice every 12 seconds and is visible for 35km on a clear night. The lens is 3.6m in diameter and contains 210 separate glass prisms and reflectors.

sedimentary rock formed horizontally under the sea and uplifted and tilted over time.

The islets and rocky shoreline attract a wide range of marine life because of their proximity to good feeding grounds. The New Zealand fur seal or kekeno will be immediately obvious. The breeding colony here numbers some 500, one of the largest on mainland New Zealand. Two other seal species frequent this place, although in small numbers only – New Zealand sea lions or pakake, and elephant seals. Nugget Point is the only place on mainland New Zealand where the three species co-exist.

Forty bird species have been recorded at Nugget Point. Seabirds abound. Besides the common red-

LEFT: Nugget Point's natural history is poetically expressed through a set of panels on the walkway. **BELOW:** The Nuggets off Nugget Point on a calm and sunny day.

billed and black-backed gulls, there are colonies of yellow-eyed penguins and blue penguins (kororā), and breeding populations of spotted shags (pārekareka), sooty shearwaters (tītī), Australasian gannets (tākapu) and royal spoonbills (kōtuku-ngutupapa). The heron-like spoonbills feed at estuaries along the coast.

The area north of the headland is sheltered from the sometimes gale-force south-westerly winds, and this is reflected in the sea by the presence of forests of bladder kelp up to 15m tall. The hardier bull kelp, anchored to inshore rocks by stout holdfasts, is found on the south side of the headland, and its fronds swirl madly in stormy seas. The steep walls of the islets provide a habitat for communities of sponges, coral, sea squirts, sea urchins and jewel anemones.

If you are heading south from here, turn into Karoro Stream Road at Willsher Bay and rejoin the main road after 16km.

TOP: A yellow-eyed penguin nesting in coastal forest. GREG LIND
ABOVE: Islets on the south side of Nugget Point headlands are decorated by swirling fronds of bull kelp, the largest of all seaweed species. In April, the lighthouse casts its shadow on one of the islets.

OWAKA

Located on the Southern Scenic Route and 30km from Balclutha, Owaka is the modest capital of the Catlins. The population is about 330. A farming and visitor-servicing centre, Owaka has shops, cafés, motels, a hotel, backpackers' accommodation, an information centre and museum, art galleries, a medical centre, pharmacy, museum, gift shop, garage and a petrol station with 24-hour fuel. The Owaka Museum Wahi Kahuika, in Campbell Street, has an attractive fresh approach to displaying the region's history. A community gallery in the complex rotates exhibitions of arts and crafts.

Owaka has moved with the times. It was once located on the road to Pounawea, close to the navigable Owaka River, and it was also sited by Catlins Lake. It moved to its present location to meet the Catlins River branch railway. Neither ships nor trains service the town nowadays. Road transport keeps the town supplied and, in turn, Owaka can supply just about all a traveller might need.

Owaka Museum features the maritime and shipwreck history of the Catlins.

Tunnel Hill Historic Reserve near Owaka.

CATLINS RAILWAY

About 3km north of Owaka, adjacent to the main road, is a historic reserve featuring a 246m-long tunnel – once the most southerly railway tunnel in New Zealand. A short walk from the carpark near the highway, the tunnel runs under McDonald's Saddle. Completed in 1895, it was excavated by pick and shovel. Take a flashlight if you want to walk through the tunnel.

The Catlins River branch railway set out from Balclutha. Construction started in 1879. By 1896 it had reached Owaka and from there the line ran up the Catlins Valley, crossed the river at Houipapa, headed on to Tawanui then round Table Hill to Caberfeidh and the Maclennan River. The railhead, Tahakopa, was reached in 1915.

The railway is best remembered for its excursion trips. Sometimes the train would stop to let children pick blackberries or mushrooms in fields beside the line.

When the line was closed in 1971, the steel rails were lifted for scrap and the bridges dismantled.

Information panels at Catlins Lake.

Roads radiate from Owaka. One runs north-west along the Owaka Valley and leads to Clinton and Southland via Purekireki. The Southern Scenic Route continues on to Catlins Lake and a turn-off into the Catlins Valley. Other roads head for the coast, providing access to Pounawea, Surat Bay, Cannibal Bay and Jacks Bay.

Catlins Lake is really an extension of the Catlins River estuary. It is tidal, and a good place for observing wading birds. A few kilometres south of Owaka is a pull-off and information panels that explain the natural history of the lake and the human settlement history of the area.

POUNAWEA

With a permanent population of about 100 residents, Pounawea gets a boost in population in the summer holidays when the cribs (holiday cottages) and camping grounds are filled. The settlement is located on the banks of an estuary fed by the Owaka and Catlins rivers. In the early 1900s a two-storey boarding house provided stylish accommodation for Dunedin business folk and other well-off holidaymakers. Fresh flounder was often served for breakfast after you were awakened by a 'dawn chorus' of bird calls. The boarding house burned down in 1917, however: you will have to catch your own flounder in the estuary these days. There are camping grounds and motor camp facilities at Pounawea, and bush and estuary walking tracks.

One track follows the banks of the Owaka River, and a longer track sets out out from the Pounawea Motor Camp and passes through tall native forest, salt meadow shrubland and saltmarsh. Allow 45 minutes to get around this track, but note that at high tide the saltmarsh portion of the track is impassable and you will need to retrace your steps through the forest. There is a shorter option, a loop track branching off after about 5 minutes, which takes you back into the settlement. Logged in the early days of European settlement, the forest is

regenerating well and there are numerous large rimu, tōtara and kahikatea in the 38ha reserve. Native forest birds are abundant, and in summer look out for migratory godwits on the saltmarsh as well as royal spoonbills and white-faced herons feeding on the tidal flats.

SURAT AND CANNIBAL BAYS

On the road between Owaka and Pounawea there is a turnoff to Surat Bay (the bridge here crosses the Owaka River). The bay is essentially a sandy beach on the north side of the estuary – and a favourite haul-out place for sea lions. Considerably larger than fur seals, the sea lions are mostly young males, some of

TOP: Saltmarsh and adjoining forest at the edge of the estuary at Pounawea. A popular walkway traverses both forest and saltmarsh. **ABOVE**: A Surat Bay sign warns of sea lions on the beach.

TOP: Surat Bay awash with breakers. Cannibal Bay is beyond and False Islet to the right. LOU SANSON

ABOVE LEFT: A male New Zealand sea lion, probably about six years old and not fully grown, at Surat Bay.

False Islet is in the background. FERGUS SUTHERLAND

ABOVE RIGHT: A southern elephant seal at Nugget Point. LOU SANSON

NEW ZEALAND SEA LION

Endemic to the New Zealand region, with most breeding occurring at the subantarctic Auckland Islands, these sea lions are making a comeback on mainland New Zealand. The Catlins coast and Otago Peninsula are attracting the most animals. Breeding in both areas dates from the mid-1990s.

On mainland New Zealand the sea lions were greatly reduced in number by early Māori hunters. Sea lion bones disappear from archaeological sites in the 17th century.

Bulls can weigh over 400kg, twice the weight of fur seal males, and they reach maturity at about eight years of age. Most of the sea lions arriving on the mainland coast from the subantarctic are sub-adult males. Surat Bay is a stronghold for them on the Catlins coast, although they are also often seen at Cannibal Bay.

Unlike fur seals, sea lions prefer to haul out on sand rather than on rocks. When ashore for long periods, they hunker down in the sand and flick it over their backs with their flippers to keep cool.

whom will have journeyed from their breeding grounds in the subantarctic Auckland Islands. Unlike fur seals, they are not afraid of humans. Keep at least 20m away from them. Highly mobile on sandy beaches, they may challenge you with a hearty roar.

Surat Bay was named after an immigrant sailing ship of 1000 tons that was beached here and became a total wreck after striking rocks farther south along the coast in 1874. About 100 of her passengers were put ashore from the stricken ship at Jacks Bay, which then made for nearby Surat Bay under full sail. No lives were lost.

It is possible to walk through dunelands to Cannibal Bay and False Islet, which is the prominent headland, but look out for snoozing sea lions in the dune vegetation. There is road access to Cannibal Bay off the Southern Scenic Route a few kilometres north of Owaka. Cannibal Bay was misnamed by geologist James Hector following the discovery of human bones in the dunes last century. The site was subsequently shown to be a Māori burial ground.

JACKS BAY AND BLOWHOLE

About 10km from Owaka, Jacks Bay is on the south side of the Catlins/Owaka estuary. You can get there by taking a side road off the road to Pounawea and crossing a bridge where the estuary narrows, or you can go the longer way around Catlins Lake.

You will pass the Owaka Yacht Club headquarters on the banks of the estuary, formerly the site of a large nineteenth-century sawmill – Guthrie and Larnach's Big Mill, built in 1871. Up to 70 men were employed, and on a busy day there could be four or five vessels loading timber here. The area is now a recreation reserve. Piles of stones close inshore are historic. They were used as ballast and offloaded by the timber vessels.

Jacks Bay is another sandy beach, staked out with cribs. From here you can walk to a popular natural feature – Jacks Blowhole. The walk across farmland takes about 30 minutes one way. The 55m-deep blowhole was formed when part of the roof of a sea cavern collapsed, leaving an opening that measures roughly 140m by 70m. Its distance from the sea is impressive – about 100m. The blowhole performs best at high tide in stormy weather. In recent years Forest and Bird volunteers and school groups have planted out the fringe surrounding the blowhole.

TUHAWAIKI ISLAND

At the south end of Jacks Bay is Tuhawaiki Island, named in honour of a 19th-century paramount chief of the southern Māori people. Tuhawaiki led his people in several battles against the celebrated North Island chief Te Rauparaha. He is best remembered in this area for a skirmish at False Islet. Finding himself trapped, he dived into the sea and swam 8km south to the island that now bears his name, also known as Jacks Island.

CATLINS RIVER

If you want to experience the Catlins hinterland, the middle and upper reaches of the Catlins River provide an outstanding opportunity. There are picnic and camping areas, walking tracks in the bush, good fishing and some interesting birdlife.

About 3km south of Catlins Lake there is a turn-off to Tawanui, an old sawmilling town 19km from Owaka. Here the Department of Conservation maintains a riverside camping area (self-registration), with toilets and a water supply. Forestry roads wind into the hills but are not recommended for camper vans or two-wheel-drive cars. Gates may be locked due to forestry operations.

There is road access all the way up the valley to The Wisp, a wonderfully evocative name for a farm lease that was taken up in 1857 by James Brugh, where there is a picnic area beside the river. For experienced trampers a route heads out via Thisbe Stream and Calliope Saddle to the headwaters of the Maclennan River, but most trampers (and anglers, for that matter) come here to use the Catlins River track. It takes about 5 hours to walk one way between Tawanui and The Wisp, a distance of 12km. The track keeps close to the river all the way, and you can join it at two points. The section between Wallis Stream and Franks Creek (1.5 hours) is especially attractive. It traverses pure silver beech forest and a gorge through which the river churns and

tumbles. There are several swing bridges along the way.

While walking the Catlins River track look out for the colourful forest songster, the canary-yellow mōhua. The birds often move about in family groups, chattering melodiously. Yellow-crowned parakeets or kākāriki sometimes accompany them. Mōhua are a threatened species and the Catlins population is out on its own.

Fitter, well-equipped trampers able to camp overnight might like to do a 24km circuit beginning and ending at Tawanui, with The Wisp the halfway point. From The Wisp's picnic ground and toilet, the higher-altitude 5-hour route back to Tawanui follows forestry roads, with a detour to a spectacular viewpoint high up, cloud permitting, at Rocky Knoll.

LEFT TOP: A fine day on Rocky Knoll, high point on the Catlins River–Wisp loop tramp. FERGUS SUTHERLAND. **RIGHT:** Catlins River is probably the most popular river in the region for recreation. **LEFT:** Kahikatea trees on lowland near the Catlins River.

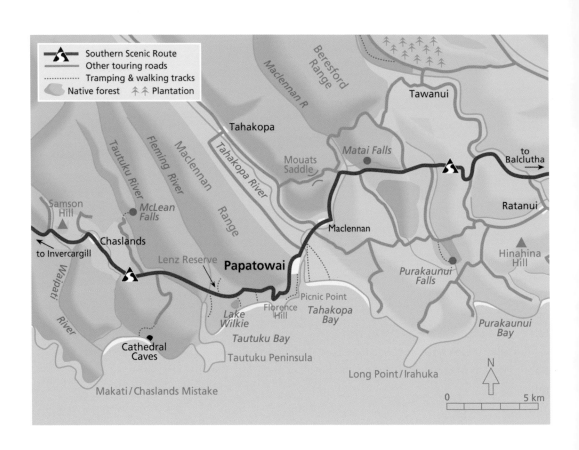

Southern Scenic Route
Other touring roads
Tramping & walking tracks
Native forest   ⼊⼊ Plantation

Beresford Range

Maclennan R

Tawanui

Tahakopa

Tahakopa River

Matai Falls

to Balclutha

Mouats Saddle

Ratanui

Maclennan Range

Fleming River

Tautuku River

Samson Hill

McLean Falls

Maclennan

Chaslands

Lenz Reserve

Papatowai

Hinahina Hill

to Invercargill

Waipati River

Purakaunui Falls

Picnic Point

Florence Hill

Tahakopa Bay

Lake Wilkie

Purakaunui Bay

Cathedral Caves

Tautuku Bay

Tautuku Peninsula

Long Point/Irahuka

N

Makati/Chaslands Mistake

0   5 km

3
THE CENTRE

THE HEART OF THE CATLINS is a breath of fresh air, clean, green and invigorating. The rainforest closes in, the valleys seem more compressed, and you really do feel you have arrived somewhere special. Besides the imposing scenery, the central zone is crowded with particular features of interest for visitors. It is a case of one enticing signpost after another.

Papatowai, right in the middle and 28km from Owaka, is the only settlement in the Central Catlins with a shop and 24hr petrol.

Between Catlins Lake and Papatowai you can detour off the highway and take an unsealed road that runs more or less parallel to the highway but closer to the coast. This provides access to the best-known waterfall in the Catlins, the Purakaunui Falls. In fact, Central Catlins begins and ends with waterfalls. Purakaunui and Matai falls are at the northern or Otago end; the McLean Falls are at the western or Southland end.

PURAKAUNUI FALLS

To get to Purakaunui Falls (17km south of Owaka), turn off the main road on the south side of the Catlins River bridge and follow the signs. There is a good-sized carpark, picnic area and toilet block opposite the track entrance.

The falls, which have long been a scenic trademark of the Catlins, are found within Purakaunui Falls Scenic Reserve on the Purakaunui River. The walking track, about 10 minutes one way, is an easy grade and suitable for wheelchairs as far as the upper lookout. You walk beside the river through impressive podocarp/beech forest. Some trees and shrubs are labelled. The track takes you to the head of the falls then descends by way of a wooden staircase to a lower viewing platform. Here you can obtain a view that has graced a postage stamp, a telephone directory and several books. The river falls about 20m in three distinct steps, each one decorated with minor cascades and the whole set framed and overhung by the forest. In normal flows the tumbling water appears silvery; in floods it is naturally browner due to staining from forest-floor tannin and organic material. In summer the falls are best photographed in mid-morning, as the afternoon sun tends to cast shadows across them.

The river meets the sea at Purakaunui Bay. There is a turn-off to Purakaunui Bay and Long Point about 4km north of the falls on the road from Ratanui. Greasy after a wet spell and dusty in dry weather, the road to Purakaunui Bay is narrow and challenging to travellers unused to gravel roads, but the bay itself is a visual treat. Cliffs rise imposingly to the north, white with encrusting lichen. The sand is fine and a creamy-buff colour, and sea lions are sometimes seen here. Toilets and a water supply are available at a picnic area and self-registering Department of Conservation campsite. People seeking a relatively quiet Catlins beach will enjoy this bay.

The road to Long Point turns off a few kilometres back from the bay. It leads to a carpark and information panel pointing out Helena Falls Bay, part of the Long Point/Irahuka Reserve, which was purchased by the Yellow-eyed Penguin Trust in 2009 for the conservation of penguins, other wildlife and the coastal ecosystem. There is no camping here and dogs cannot be taken onto the reserve or the beach.

MATAI FALLS

Smaller than Purakaunui Falls but a delightful sight nonetheless are the Matai Falls, which can be walked to in 20 minutes from the main road, 19km south of Owaka. The path to these falls is steeper at the beginning than that to Purakaunui Falls, but it soon levels out and becomes an easy stroll through forest that features avenues of native tree fuchsia or kōtukutuku – a sign of a damp environment. The forest here is protected in Table Hill Scenic Reserve.

LEFT: Matai Falls in flood. **ABOVE:** A large specimen of tree fuchsia on the Matai Falls walkway.

A wooden platform built into the bouldery bed of the stream provides a convenient place from which to view or photograph the 10m-high falls, which are neatly framed by forest. About 50m upstream this small river drops over the Horseshoe Falls, which are worth the steep five-minute climb to them when the river is running high.

Matai Rail Trail

About halfway along the Matai Falls track you can take a five-minute detour to the Matai Rail Trail, a walkway that utilises a section of the old Catlins River branch railway. The line was completed in 1915 and closed in 1971. The 2km walkway was a joint venture by Catlins Promotions and the Department of Conservation and was opened in 2015 – 100 years after the line's closure. For more than half of the twentieth century the line was the main means of transport for Catlins goods, produce and people. It averaged a 1-in-40 gradient through the walkway section, one of the steepest railway gradients in the South Island, but it is an easy walk through impressive cuttings and regenerating forest. The story of the railway is well told in a

A deep sandstone cutting near the eastern end of the Matai Rail Trail.

sequence of illustrated information panels. The walk uphill from where the access track meets the rail corridor takes about 30 minutes one way; the downhill section takes 10 minutes and passes through a cutting of Arenite sandstone up to 10m deep, constructed by railway gangs using explosives, wheelbarrows, picks and shovels.

From the highway in the Matai Falls area there are views inland to Table Hill, which looks as its name suggests – flat on top. From the sea the hill also cuts a distinctive profile, and served as a landmark for shipping in the early days. More adventurous motorists can skirt around Table Hill Scenic Reserve by way of a back road that does as well as any to make you feel you are off the beaten track. The northern extension of this back road links up with Tawanui. Take your time; it is not a road for high speeds.

The Maclennan River emerges from its lofty forested headwaters at Caberfeidh, a name that honours an early member of parliament, Thomas Mackenzie. Caberfeidh is a traditional name of Scotland's Clan Mackenzie.

The next point of interest heading south is the settlement of Maclennan, located where the river empties into an estuary that is also fed by the Tahakopa River. Maclennan, across the

A patchwork of multiple land uses in the Tahakopa Valley: sheep, a swathe of indigenous forest and plantation forestry with introduced tree species.

estuary from Papatowai, is named for the first runholder in the Tahakopa Valley, Murdoch Maclennan, who arrived in 1884. The village once buzzed with sawmill and railway activity but is a quiet place today, especially since the closure of the store and post office.

The Maclennan and Tahakopa valleys once had numerous dairy farms that supplied a dairy factory at Owaka. Sheep and cattle are farmed today, with pasture having been developed on land cleared largely by bulldozers. The first bulldozers arrived in the district in the 1940s.

Across two one-lane bridges lies Papatowai, Tautuku Bay and some magnificent rainforest and coastal wilderness. The Maclennan River bridge was built in 1916; the bridge across the Tahakopa River estuary was completed in 1921.

By the Maclennan bridge a side road (Puaho Road) provides access to the Purakaunui Falls area. Where this road climbs above the Tahakopa Bay dune forest there is a viewpoint over one of the few tracts of dense lowland podocarp forest to survive the milling era.

Another road from near the Maclennan bridge heads inland up the Tahakopa Valley and leads to what was once a busy sawmilling centre and the railway terminus at the settlement of Tahakopa. It is the route to eastern Southland (Wyndham, 64km) via Mokoreta.

South of Papatowai the next townships are Waikawa (38km) and Tokanui (53km).

PAPATOWAI

At picturesque Papatowai, 28km from Owaka, the Southern Scenic Route brings you within earshot of the sea. There is salt in the air. From their perch on the south bank of the Tahakopa estuary, the residences and holiday homes of Papatowai look out over the winding estuary and Tahakopa Bay Scenic Reserve forest. Many of the houses are nestled among trees, which attract large, colourful New Zealand pigeons that spend hours feeding on favoured fruits, flowers and leaves. Pigeons are keen on kōwhai, the flowers and young leaves of fuchsia and, in autumn, the fruit of any of the podocarp trees, especially rimu, kahikatea and miro.

At weekends in summer and during school holidays, Papatowai's small population swells with visitors. Over the years the township has grown to meet the needs of visitors.

Papatowai offers a variety of accommodation and a store (groceries, food, alcoholic beverages, postal services, petrol), and has a playground and a large picnic area, with toilet block, adjacent to the beach and estuary.

Parked by the highway at Papatowai is the Lost Gypsy Gallery, a bus and adjacent outdoor space jam-packed with amusing and wacky inventions featuring found objects – a wildly delightful distraction from all the natural wonders. Blair Somerville is the mastermind behind the

mechanical gadgetry. He opened his free-entry stationary bus in 1999 and his Winding Thoughts Theatre, for which there is a fee, in 2008. Coffee and food carts have since joined the gypsy milieu. The gallery is closed through the winter months.

Visitors who pass through Papatowai without stopping will miss the essence of the Catlins. There are enough walks and attractions here and in the next bay south, Tautuku, to keep a fit person busy for a couple of days. Social events include, on New Year's Eve, a 'big dig' on the beach for children during the day and a bonfire in the evening. Another annual event, which started in 1997, is the Papatowai Challenge, a 15.5km walk/run on bush tracks, beaches and rural roads in late February or early March, involving as many as 400 participants. Visitors are welcome to join in. Proceeds from the entry fee go to charitable causes.

TOP LEFT: The beach near Picnic Point, Papatowai. TOP RIGHT: Kings Rock, destination of an extension of the Picnic Point track. An earthquake toppled the pillar in 2007. ABOVE: Big surf: a body boarder catches one of the waves for which the Catlins is renowned. ISABELLA HARREX

Papatowai walks

One of the most popular walks in the Catlins is the Picnic Point track – a walk for all seasons and ages. The circuit, involving beach and forest, takes about 40 minutes and can be walked in either direction. Setting

Tahakopa estuary at low tide, opposite Papatowai. Across the river is the Tahakopa dune forest. The Old Coach Road track leads to the forest near the mouth.

out from the picnic ground, follow the shoreline as it curves around to Picnic Point. The views are of one of the least-modified sections of coast in the Catlins. If the tide is out there are rock pools to explore.

At Picnic Point, you pick up the track back to the township through the forest. The entrance from the beach is marked by a sign commemorating a well-known Papatowai artist, Edna May Peterson, who died in 1989 aged 82. The forest walk is evenly graded and emerges at Papatowai's upper road. Large rimu and mataī trees top a canopy of kamahi and rātā. The understorey is rich in ferns and perching plants, and often tangled by supplejack vines.

A few metres from the Edna Peterson memorial the track forks, with the main branch heading back to Papatowai and the other path bound for Kings Rock. Allow an hour for the round trip to Kings Rock. The going gets steeper but is well worth the effort. After negotiating more forest you reach open farmland. Follow the markers across the pasture (and a gully that can be muddy when wet) to rejoin the coast near Kings Rock, which lost its eye-catching pillar in an earthquake in 2007. The rocky shoreline is full of intertidal life.

A relatively new walkway, close to the village centre, is Shanks Bush Nature Walk (20

Papatowai rainforest, dense as any jungle.

minutes) at the intersection of Tahakopa Valley Road and the highway. Its winding track loops through a piece of regenerating estuarine coastal forest and shrubland featuring a grove of young kahikatea (white pine) trees. Of special interest to families with young children, numerous educational and interactive novelties are dotted along the track.

Across the estuary from Papatowai is the Old Coach Road track which, as its name suggests, follows a coastal track built for early horse-drawn transport. The track begins on the north side of the Tahakopa River bridge and follows the curve of the estuary to the ocean beach (30 minutes one way). The coaches, incidentally, forded the river just downstream of the present bridge.

As well as its podocarp component the forest here is notable for its silver beech trees, the most southerly in the country. Near the river mouth is a stand of young tōtara trees. They mark an important archaeological site – an early Māori moa hunters' encampment of several hundred years ago. During numerous excavations over the years archaeologists have unearthed stone knives, adzes, bone fish hooks and other artefacts, together with moa bones in ancient middens.

Fitter walkers have a choice at this point. They can continue along the beach and pick up a track back through the forest to the Old Coach Road and carpark (allow about 3 hours for the round trip), or they can go on further and climb the hill at the far end of the beach, from where the route leads to back roads (Ratanui and Sharks Creek Roads) and finally Puaho Road and the way back to Maclennan and the carpark. The longer circuit, a distance of about 12km, takes more than half a day.

TAUTUKU

The name Tautuku is synonymous with the wilderness character of the Catlins coast. About 2km south of Papatowai you can take it all in at the Florence Hill lookout, where there is an array of information panels. Before you lies Tautuku Bay's crescent of sand with Tautuku Peninsula and its lonely cribs in the distance, and the whole vista of wave-wrinkled ocean and hilly landscape backed by continuous forest. No road leads to the cribs, and getting there can be an adventure. The owners use tractors and four-wheel-drive vehicles to ford the Tautuku River at low tide.

If you were here in 1839 you would have been looking across to a whaling station near the neck of the peninsula, established by William Palmer for Johnny Jones. When Otago's first surveyor, Frederick Tuckett, visited the area in 1844 he found the whalers living in 'comfortable little cottages'. They had 'cleared and cultivated some ten acres of land, on which were grown

View of Tautuku Bay from Florence Hill.

OUTDOOR EXPERIENCE

For more than 40 years Tautuku Lodge (formerly known as the Tautuku Outdoor Education Centre) has been introducing school children and adults to the natural wonders of the Catlins. Following decades of catering for school groups for up to five days at a time, Tautuku Lodge now also hosts pre-arranged groups of trampers.

The Otago Youth Adventure Trust, formed in 1968, built the complex in 1975 with the assistance of scores of volunteers. Activities for school groups include walks and tramps, kayaking, a flying fox and confidence course. Natural history and conservation figure largely in the studies.

TAUTUKU FOREST CABINS

Self-catering accommodation suitable for individuals or groups can be booked at the Forest and Bird organisation's Tautuku Forest Cabins on Lenz Reserve, 8km south of Papatowai. Visitors need to bring their own sleeping bags and food. For booking enquiries, see: www.forestandbird.org. nz/what-we-do/lodges/Tautuku-Lodge-Otago. Alternatively, go to Facebook.com/Catlins-forest-cabins-Tautuku.

An aerial view of Tautuku Bay from the south, with the Tautuku River mouth and Tautuku Peninsula cribs in the foreground.
LOU SANSON

wheat, barley, and potatoes. They also had ducks, fowl and goats.' The whalers stayed for about seven years (during which some 50 whales were caught), and the port was later developed to serve the timber, flax and fishing industries. It is no longer a port.

From the Florence Hill lookout you can just see the roofs of a group of buildings peeping out of the forest near the bottom of the hill. This is Tautuku Lodge, a centre with a long history of outdoor education and experience for school groups (see panel p. 44). In the distance are the densely forested gullies cut by the Fleming and Tautuku rivers.

Off to the left is a little island, a wildlife sanctuary where a blowhole (Rere Kohu or Spouting Cave) sends forth spray that lights up as a rainbow in

certain conditions. There is a good view of Rainbow Isles from the beach, which can be reached by an access road that leads off from State Highway 92 at the bottom of the hill. Note the size of the rimu in this area, which is part of the 480ha William King Scenic Reserve. King, recognised for his love of the native forest and its bird life, came from a pioneering family who farmed on Florence Hill.

Tautuku walks

Instead of driving to the beach, try an easy walk through the Tautuku dune forest from the highway. The track entrance is opposite Tautuku Lodge. Allow about 15 minutes each way.

About 150m from the start of the walkway you will find two podocarps of medium size standing side by side – a tōtara and a miro. They are worth hugging. This forest was protected in 1902.

When you get to the beach you have the option of doing a circuit north along the beach to the access road and thus back to the track entrance on the highway. Near where the access road meets the beach are Isas Cave and Isas Creek.

About 500m south of the dune forest walk is a scenic gem – Lake Wilkie. Just 100m from the highway and 400m from the beach, the lake has much to teach us about the way plant life surrounding a wetland of this kind is slowly transformed into forest. Information panels explain the process of forest succession and the plant zonings, from small wetland plants, through a shrub

TOP: Lake Wilkie, Tautuku. The vegetation grades from small wetland plants at the edge of the lake through shrubland to tall forest.
LEFT: Lake Wilkie boardwalk and information panels. **OPPOSITE:** The boardwalk through jointed rushes at Tautuku estuary.

FERNBIRD

At Tautuku estuary and the wetland areas of Lenz Reserve, keep an eye out for the South Island fernbird, a threatened native species. The Tautuku area is a stronghold for it.

Small and brownish, the fernbird or mātātā may be seen flying weakly over the rushes and wetland shrubs, with its tail dangling. You are more likely to hear its metallic chirrups than to see the bird in the air, however.

The fernbird nests low down in wetland vegetation through spring and summer.

zone on deep peat, to tall forest. In the process the lake is slowly filling in. It is known as a 'bog lake', occupying a natural hollow in the dunes.

The path starts out through a showcase stand of mature rimu trees then leads down to a boardwalk at the lake edge, which you can reach in little more than five minutes from the carpark. In summer look out for little whistling frogs clinging to the blades of flax at the lake shore. When the rātā trees are flowering well, the forest canopy fringing Lake Wilkie turns a spectacular red.

About 1.5km south of Lake Wilkie – and 7km from Papatowai – is another short walkway to Tautuku estuary, where a boardwalk allows easy access to meadows of jointed rushes at the edge of the estuary. Fernbirds inhabit the estuarine shrubland. The track to the boardwalk takes about 10 minutes.

From the end of the boardwalk you can look across to the other side of the estuary and see how the forest to the south is taller and more intact. The forest on the north side is slowly regenerating. A prominent tree species is three-finger *Pseudopanax colensoi*, whose large leaves are arranged in sets of three. Possums eat the stems of three-finger leaves, which may account for why so many leaves lie at the foot of these trees. Possums represent a major threat to the Catlins forests, and poisoning and trapping operations are conducted to try to control their numbers.

Access to Lenz Reserve (550ha) is from the south side of the Fleming River bridge. The reserve, owned by the Forest and Bird organisation, offers an easy 150m walk ('A Walk Through

CATLINS SAWMILLING

Since the early 1860s more than 180 sawmills have operated in the Catlins. Most were small-scale ventures that lasted just a few years.

As the railway extended south from Owaka in the early 1900s, sawmills opened up to take advantage of the ready access to markets for the timber. From the 1920s, roads and lorries supplemented the trade.

In the Maclennan district in the late 1920s, logs were floated down the Maclennan River to be milled. The big Maclennan mill was destroyed by fire in September 1935, when hot, dry, gale-force north-westerly winds fanned flames across a huge area from Tahakopa to Glenomaru.

The boom years for Catlins sawmilling were 1919–29 and 1940–55. At times 30 mills were operating in the region. As the native forest was cleared, farms were developed on the better land, and the less-fertile land was allowed to revert to bush.

ABOVE: George Clarke's Tautuku sawmill operated from 1901 to 1911. This photograph was taken about 1902. Single men's huts are at right. A steam engine was transported from Canterbury to drive the mill. It reached Owaka by rail and from there was towed south by a bullock team – a journey that took seven days. The Clarke family had a scow built to ship timber to Dunedin from Tautuku. Towards the end of its life the mill had different owners, including Sir Truby King of Plunket fame. All the big podocarp species were milled – rimu, mataī, kahikatea, tōtara and miro.
DON JENKS COLLECTION

ABOVE LEFT: Hound's tongue fern.
ABOVE: The Tautuku Forest Cabins on Lenz Reserve. **LEFT**: The Traills tractor hauled wagons loaded with logs through the Tautuku bush.

Time') to the Traills tractor and bush tramway exhibit and, for fitter walkers, the 1-hour loop Nature and Tramway Walk that accesses part of the reserve on the adjacent hill. Plaques along the old tramways identify trees and explain the history of logging and log transport here.

The tractor, a Fordson farm tractor converted for use on wooden rails, was the invention of Frank Traills, a Southland sawmiller, who took out a patent for it in 1924. The machine replaced horse-drawn trams on steeper country, pushing and pulling wagons loaded with logs. To pay its way, the Dunedin-manufactured Traills tractor was required to deliver six logs a day. A total of 36 tractors were sold in the 12 years to 1936.

Operations of this sort ceased in 1952. Sawmilling in the Catlins was in decline from the mid-1950s.

ABOVE: Cathedral Caves. SIMON NOBLE/DOC RIGHT: McLean Falls

CATHEDRAL CAVES

A striking feature of the region's coastline, the Cathedral Caves attract visitors to lonely Waipati Beach, 15km south of Papatowai. The main caves comprise two passages that together measure 200m and up to 30m in height. Access is available during daylight hours between late October and May and is restricted to two hours before and one hour after low tide. Before setting out check the day's tide timetables at the information centres at Owaka or Waikawa or online at www.cathedralcaves.co.nz.

The access road leads off the highway about 2km south of the bridge over the Tautuku River. From the carpark the walking track through indigenous forest to the beach crosses Māori and Department of Conservation land. There is a small charge to cover maintenance of the access road and walking track. It takes about 20 minutes to walk to the beach and another 10 minutes to reach the caves.

As sea water can pool inside the caves, you might like to walk barefoot – it will enhance your experience of the amazing natural sculpture. A flashlight is recommended for use in the dimly lit inner reaches. Admire the tenacity of the ferns growing from the bare-rock ceiling.

Formed by wave action over eons, the caves were named by Dr T.M. Hocken in 1896 because of their cathedral-like character. Dr Hocken's party tried out the caves' acoustic effects – what he termed their 'reverberating qualities … full test being made by whistling, singing and coo-eeing'.

Around the corner is a smaller set of caves that may attract the bolder, more agile visitor. Watch out for rogue waves, though.

The Cathedral Caves are occasionally closed to visitors because of rough sea conditions or unsuitable tides. At such times, signs are posted at the access-road gate and at information centres.

McLEAN FALLS

The tallest of the waterfalls in the Catlins is McLean Falls in the middle reaches of the remarkably unmodified Tautuku River. Here the river drops 22m into a ravine and flows on through a series of cascades, chutes and boulders.

Access is off Rewcastle Road, less than 1km south of the Cathedral Caves turn-off. North-bound travellers will come upon the turn-off soon after leaving Chaslands farm country and entering forest again. Visitor accommodation, a holiday park and the Whistling Frog Café and Bar are located close to the corner. Drive to the end of Rewcastle Road (3km) where there is a carpark and a walking track to the falls (about 40 minutes return). It winds through amazingly diverse shrubland and taller forest, featuring pepper trees (bushes with deep-red leaves), New Zealand holly (a type of tree daisy), mānuka bushes and tree ferns. The track follows the dark river for about half the way, and the last 50 metres is a rocky zig-zag climb cut into the side of the ravine.

CHASLANDS

Between the Tautuku and Waikawa areas lies Chaslands, the remotest part of the Catlins. In effect, it is a large clearing in the middle of the

A remnant patch of protected red tussock grassland in Chaslands on a rainbow day. An information kiosk describes local natural features and human history. FERGUS SUTHERLAND

A river of wool: a large mob of sheep on the Chaslands highway, being moved from a Waikawa farm to pasture in Chaslands.

Catlins forest, logged in the early 1990s then converted to farmland. Chaslands once had three sawmills, a dairy factory and school, but only the farms remain – plus visitor accommodation in the form of farm cottages that are appealing for their remote location.

Prominent above the network of cleared valley floors is Samson Hill (240m), a round peak named by an early surveyor for his dog. Once incorrectly thought to be a volcano, it was formed from vertical cracking and erosion. Samson Hill Scenic Reserve, which flanks the hill, contains many rātā trees that present spectacular colour when flowering. Plantations of exotic trees, including pines and cypresses, are slowly changing the character of the district. In the open area of Chaslands is a pull-off for vehicles and information about a red tussock restoration project. The old Chaslands cemetery is also being highlighted with a walkway and interpretation panels.

On the Waikawa side of Chaslands is Chaslands Scenic Reserve, a beautiful tract of forest topped by large rimu. Distinctive at the forest edge are kamahi, tree fuchsia, New Zealand holly, wineberry and tree ferns. You might easily mistake this forest for somewhere in South Westland.

South of Waipati Beach is a headland called Chaslands Mistake, named after an Australian, Tommy Chaseland, who came to southern New Zealand in the 1820s for the whaling and sealing and stayed for 45 years. His piloting skills on the south-east coast became legendary. The schooner *Wallace* (1866) and steamer *Otago* (1876) were wrecked near the point.

In Chaslands forest is the boundary between Otago and Southland, and west of here lie the extensive farmlands of the Waikawa Valley where the countryside, compared to that of Chaslands, looks and feels more developed.

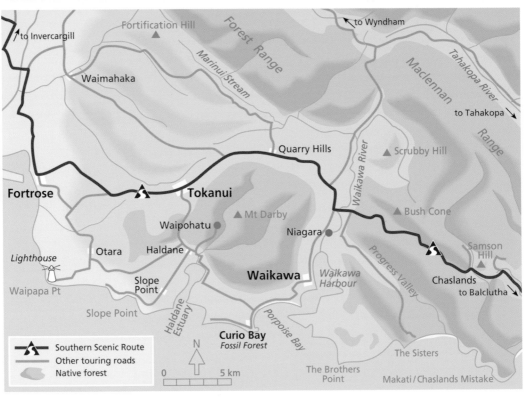

4

THE SOUTH

WAIKAWA VALLEY marks a change in the Catlins landform. The north-west 'grain' in the ranges and valleys runs out here; to the south and west lies a more jumbled landscape. The Catlins forest flows on south and west of Waikawa as far as the Tokanui area. Waikawa strongly identifies with Southland. Its transport, economic and social links are mostly with Southland; yet there is a geographical connection with Otago through the Catlins.

Just west of the Waikawa River bridge is a T-junction. Travellers from the north turn left for Niagara, Waikawa, Porpoise Bay, Curio Bay and the coastal route to Fortrose, and right for the inland route through Tokanui to Fortrose. A short distance inland from the junction a side road climbs to the head of the Waikawa Valley, taking you to Mokoreta, Wyndham and Gore.

The coastal route, although longer, is full of interest. Niagara, close to where the Waikawa River flows into its broad estuary, was named by someone who had seen North America's Niagara Falls and thought the rapids on the lower Waikawa – mere ripples at high tide – deserved ironic recognition as the world's smallest waterfall. It is visible upstream of the bridge at Niagara. In 1901 Niagara was a bustling sawmill town with its own school, post office and library. The school became a church, then a dance hall, then a pottery, and in the 1990s was transformed into an award-winning restaurant.

At Waikawa, which is on the same line of latitude as Bluff, you are close to the bottom of the South Island. Visitors stream through Waikawa in summer. The main focus for the area today is the Waikawa

TOP LEFT: The wharf at Waikawa Harbour.
RIGHT: St Mary's Anglican Church, Waikawa.

and Districts Museum and Information Centre, 6km from the turn-off, 56km from Owaka. It is open daily, offering visitor information and exhibiting relics from the sawmilling and whaling eras. The museum also owns the picturesque little St Mary's Anglican Church across the road. It was opened in March 1932 and closed in 1994. A roadside café opposite specialises in meals of blue cod. A delightful 20-minute harbourside walk through native forest, the George Aitken track, starts behind the Waikawa Hall.

The Waikawa whaling base (1838–43) was on the other side of the harbour, just inside North Head, but as the timber trade grew and sheep farms produced wool for export, the settlement moved to the south side. The population around the harbour today is about 50, with farming, tourism and fishing the main pursuits. Several commercial fishing vessels use the jetties that extend into the tidal stream. At spring tides the water flowing past the jetties can reach five knots, causing the vessels to strain at their mooring lines. The tidal range is 3m.

Including the Porpoise Bay–Curio Bay area, the district now boasts a wide range of visitor accommodation, with a total of about 200 beds available in motels, beach cottages, backpacker lodges, farmstays and homestays – a centre of southern hospitality.

If you like collecting landmarks, you might ask the way to Slope Point (see page 61), the southernmost point on the South Island – about 7km further south than Bluff. Waipapa Point,

Porpoise Bay from the headland that also overlooks Curio Bay.

more commonly visited than Slope Point, is often mistaken as the bottom of the South Island.

PROGRESS VALLEY

For an out-of-the-way experience, take the Progress Valley Road to Dummys Beach and Long Beach, situated on the coast about halfway between Waikawa Harbour and Waipati Beach. The unsealed road, best travelled in dry weather, is accessible from Niagara and also from the highway on the Chaslands side of the Waikawa junction.

This part of the coast was a busy little goldmining centre in the 1870s and through to the turn of the century. In the early 1900s a system of water races was built to generate power.

PORPOISE BAY

Waikawa Harbour meets the ocean at Porpoise Bay, 2km south of the information centre. The bay is inhabited by the delightful little Hector's dolphins, the world's smallest marine dolphin. It is a threatened species. Summer is when the dolphins are mainly seen playing in the surf. The bay's long arc of golden sand stretches from South Head to the harbour entrance. The southern end is well protected from southerly swells, which may be why the dolphins find it so attractive. The beach sands were mined for gold in the nineteenth century, and as recently as the 1980s on a limited scale.

HECTOR'S DOLPHINS

From the Curio Bay area and the beach at Porpoise Bay you may catch sight of Hector's dolphins swimming just outside the breaker line in Porpoise Bay. The rounded dorsal fin breaks the surface when they breath. Visitors are warned not to approach the dolphins – let them come to you.

Hector's dolphins, the world's smallest species (about 1.4m long) and one of the rarest, do not leap out of the water as often as, say, dusky dolphins, which are also found on the southern coasts. Hector's dolphins are paler than most other dolphin species – light grey to white.

They stay fairly close to shore and are not known to travel far from home waters. The nearest population to the Porpoise Bay group is based in Te Waewae Bay on the south coast near Fiordland. Porpoise Bay can have as many as 30 dolphins in several pods swimming around at any one time. Mother and calf combinations are fairly common, suggesting that Porpoise Bay is a nursery area. In winter most of the dolphins disperse to destinations unknown. They feed on small fish such as yellow-eyed mullet and ahuru.

ABOVE: Hector's dolphins romping in Porpoise Bay surf. NICK SMART/CATLINS SURF SCHOOL

CURIO BAY

Curio Bay, around the corner from Porpoise Bay and about 75km from Owaka and 90km from Invercargill, is the South Catlins' best-known attraction. Together with Nugget Point (North Catlins) and Purakaunui Falls (Central Catlins) it has achieved icon status. It helps to have a catchy name, of course, but Curio Bay by any other name would still attract visitors because of its fossil forest – a geological wonder that excites a steady procession of visitors every year.

The road to Curio Bay curves around Porpoise Bay with its row of waterfront homes, visitor accommodation and information centre. From here a short path leads to a viewing platform overlooking the southern part of Curio Bay and a staircase down to the shoreline.

At low tide the fossil forest is spectacularly exposed on an intertidal rock platform as petrified logs and stumps, an astonishing 160 million years old. Some of the trunks measure over 20m in length. They represent Jurassic-age conifer trees

THIS PAGE AND OPPOSITE: When the tide is out a rock platform at Curio Bay displays fossil logs, stumps and pieces of petrified wood from the age of dinosaurs.

TOP: The sign at the entrance to the forest walk and rock platform at Curio Bay (BOTTOM).

similar to Norfolk pines and kauri. No birds flew in this forest, for birds had yet to evolve. Nor were there any flowering trees. Tuatara-like reptiles existed, however, together with frogs, insects and dinsoaurs. Volcanic ash and mud flows buried the forest and over the eons the wood was replaced by silica in a fossilising process that made the logs resistant to the powerful erosive forces of the sea. Growth rings measured in the silicified wood indicate a climate that had distinct seasons.

Please do not souvenir any fossils – even the smallest fragments. This is a natural work of art of international importance.

The forest and shrubland backing onto Curio Bay provides nesting habitat for a small and vulnerable population of yellow-eyed penguins. Take care not to disturb them.

Across the road from the cliff-top viewing platform is a 15-minute walkway through podocarp forest, the Curio Bay Tumu Toka Walkway. The forest is remarkable for its dense stand of young rimu trees and tall mānuka.

MARINE RESERVES

Protection of parts of the Catlins coastal marine environment has been in the minds of local people for some years, whether they are in support of such proposals or opposed to them. From 2014–17 a government-appointed body, the Southeast Marine Protection Forum, worked on developing proposals for marine reserves and other kinds of marine protected areas between Timaru and Waipapa Point. Twenty proposals were issued for public comment in October 2016 with a view to the forum making recommendations to the government by the end of 2017. Five of the 20 proposals were for parts of the Catlins coastal and estuarine areas, notably a marine reserve (no take, no disturbance) along 7.5km of coastline between Pillans Head and Purakaunui Bay, with Long Point approximately the halfway mark.

POINTS WEST

Slope Point and Waipapa Point appeal as places to explore. You can turn off at Porpoise Bay and take the back road through Haldane, or, if you are approaching from Southland, there are roads from Fortrose and the Tokanui area that lead separately to these two headlands.

From Porpoise Bay the road to Slope Point loops around Haldane Bay and its estuary – an expanse of mudflats at low tide – for about 15km. On the western side of the estuary there is a camping ground (Weirs Beach Domain)

TOP: The lighthouse at Waipapa Point. Slope Point is in the distance. **ABOVE**: Not an unusual sight on the southern coast – a windshorn macrocarpa tree at Slope Point.

WRECK OF THE *TARARUA*

New Zealand's second-worst shipping tragedy occurred at Waipapa Point. On the night of 29 April 1881 the 828-ton SS *Tararua* struck Otara Reef, about 1km off the coast, in rainy conditions while on a voyage from Port Chalmers to Melbourne via Foveaux Strait. Only 20 of the 151 passengers and crew survived.

Many were drowned when the lifeboats were dashed on rocks near the shore; others stayed on the stricken wreck overnight but died when the pounding seas finally toppled the masts and capsized the hull of the ship. The captain was among those who died. A court of inquiry found fault in his navigation and he was further blamed for not posting a proper lookout.

Most of the victims are buried in a plot now known as the Tararua Acre, 2km down the road from the lighthouse. There are only a few headstones in the burial ground, accessed via a 300m walk from the road over farmland.

and backpacker accommodation, accessible from Slope Point Road. Cliffs and rocky reefs characterise the shoreline. Look out for the windshorn trees in the paddocks, a sign of this area's exposure to southerly gales. For an exhilarating walk in South Catlins forest, take the road to the Waipohatu Recreation Area from Haldane. An easy 30-minute walk loops from the picnic area, where there are toilets. A longer walking track through this forest reserve, passing two waterfalls, takes about 3 hours.

At Waipapa Point the land flattens out. Sandy beaches and dunes are extensive here, and the elegant lighthouse – the last wooden lighthouse built in New Zealand – stands only 21m above sea level. Offshore reefs, difficult for shipping to see, underline the importance of the light, which marks the eastern entrance to Foveaux Strait. Now automated, it is visible for 22km and flashes once every 10 seconds. It was erected in 1884 following the 1881 wreck of the screw steamer *Tararua*. On the western side of the lighthouse is a delightful little beach of coarse orange sand where the water is protected by a reef. On a clear day you can see the tall chimney of the Tiwai Point (Bluff) aluminium smelter to the west, and Stewart Island's mountains in the southwest. To the east Slope Point is about 12km distant. Late afternoon light here has a magic quality that will be appreciated by photographers. Sea lions sometimes haul out on the sand.

This logo marks the Southern Scenic Route.

5

THE SOUTHERN SCENIC ROUTE

SOUTHERN SCENIC ROUTE DISTANCES

Dunedin–Balclutha (via Taieri Mouth) 90km
Balclutha–Invercargill 162km
Invercargill–Tuatapere 88km
Tuatapere–Te Anau 108km
Te Anau–Milford Sound 120km

THE CATLINS COAST forms the eastern shoulder of the Southern Scenic Route, which swings around the bottom of the South Island, from Dunedin in the east to Fiordland (Te Anau and Milford Sound) in the west. On a map of the South Island the route mimics a large and generous smile, and many a traveller ends up smiling having completed the journey.

After the leg between the City of Dunedin and Balclutha (via the coastal settlements of Brighton and

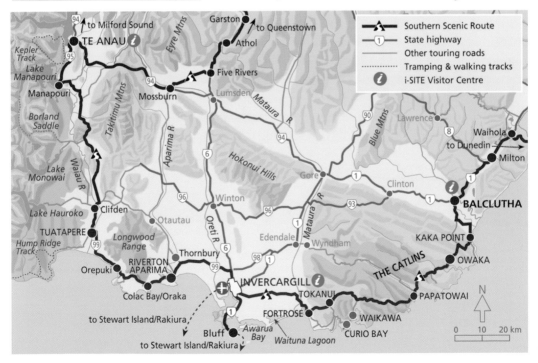

Taieri Mouth and inland Lake Waihola and Milton) there are three main components to the route – Catlins Coast, Southland Coast and Fiordland. Along the route there are numerous detour possibilities. While on the Southland Coast you can take a trip to Stewart Island by sea (1 hour by catamaran from Bluff) or by air (20 minutes in a light plane from Invercargill Airport). Several major rivers cross the plains of Southland, and the Mataura or Oreti rivers may invite further exploration, especially if angling is your favourite recreation.

In Fiordland opportunities to detour abound. They range from tramping tracks or day-walks in the Takitimu and Longwood ranges to exploration within the boundaries of Fiordland National Park.

It is possible to drive from Dunedin to Te Anau in one very long day, but such an itinerary is a waste of the myriad recreational and sightseeing opportunities.

SOUTHLAND COAST

Fortrose, at the western edge of the Catlins region, is a pleasant 45km drive from Invercargill across the coastal fringe of the Southland Plains. Fortrose is where the Mataura River reaches its estuary, the easternmost of a series of inlets and estuaries along the Southland Coast. There are picnic and camping facilities here, and a boat ramp.

Fortrose was the site of a 19th-century whaling station that was managed by the legendary Tommy Chaseland. The station started with a flurry of activity (11 whales were caught in about a fortnight) but the whales disappeared suddenly and the station was closed within two years.

As the highway veers due west towards Invercargill, several roads lead off south to penetrate an area known as Awarua Wetland or Seaward Moss, renowned for the richness of its vegetation and birdlife. Numerous streams feed into Waituna Lagoon, and a few kilometres to the east is a larger estuary, Awarua Bay, which is linked with Bluff Harbour.

You are at the outskirts of Invercargill before you know it – no matter from which direction you approach – because the city has no hills marking it. Because of the low relief, it is hard to gauge the extent of the Southland provincial capital, population about 50,000. Several of the southern suburbs are draped around the upper reaches of the largest estuary on the Southland Coast, the New River estuary.

INVERCARGILL

For information on what to do and see in Invercargill and other parts of Southland, call at the Invercargill Visitor Centre in the Southland Museum and Art Gallery at 108 Gala Street, Queens Park. The museum is a major attraction and its subantarctic gallery and live tuatara display are especially impressive. Next door is lovely Queens Park.

Riverton's life blood is the sea. It has been an important fishing port for more than 150 years.

RIVERTON

Both a river town and a seaside one, Riverton boasts the longest European history of any southern New Zealand town. Its origins date from the early 1800s when sealers and whalers were active around Foveaux Strait.

About 40km from Invercargill, Riverton lies at the mouth of an estuary fed by the Aparima and Pourakino rivers at the western end of a long arcing coastline. It is the Southland Coast's most popular seaside resort. Its beaches at Riverton Rocks and Taramea Bay are safe and popular through summer, and the river holds its own attractions for anglers and boaties.

Aparima is the Māori name for both the locality and the river, but the estuary carries the name Jacobs River, in memory of a Māori chief who was known to the whalers as Old Jacob.

An important fishing port, Riverton was established as a whaling station about 1835 by Captain John Howell. Overlooking the river mouth is a stone memorial to Howell accompanied by whalers' trypots and an anchor. Riverton was once in contention as the main port for

Colac Bay, seen from the scenic reserve behind Riverton.
WENDY HARREX

Southland, rivalling Bluff. Māori and early European history is well displayed at the redeveloped Riverton Museum, Te Hikoi Southern Journey.

You can charter jet boats here for fishing or sightseeing, and visit a factory that produces pāua-shell souvenirs. Around New Year Riverton puts on a summer carnival. Further west the Longwood Range rises invitingly for visitors more attracted to forested hills than to the sea. The Pourakino Valley on the eastern side of the Longwoods is a popular destination for bush walkers, picnickers, brown trout anglers and deer hunters. About 12km north-east of Riverton and a short distance off State Highway 99 is the little settlement of Thornbury, home of a vintage farm machinery museum.

The highway heading west from Riverton meets Colac Bay after about 6km. There is access here to a broad sandy beach, popular among surf-board riders. At the western end of the beach is Colac Bay township, a historic Māori settlement. There are outlets for local crafts and artwork. Offshore is Centre Island, marking the western entrance to Foveaux Strait, and beyond are the high hills of Stewart Island.

TUATAPERE

Self-styled as the 'sausage capital' of New Zealand, Tuatapere is actually a sawmilling centre and the gateway to southern Fiordland. It straddles the Waiau River about 10km from the mouth – a convenient place for a bridge because downstream of here the river broadens and becomes braided. Tuatapere has all the services you might expect of medium-sized town (population about 800) in a relatively remote rural area.

For decades Tuatapere's sawmills thrived on native timber from forests on either side of the Waiau Valley, but less native timber is available now and the industry is gradually converting

OREPUKI

At the eastern end of Te Waewae Bay, close to the sea cliffs and in the shadow of the Longwood Range, is the township of Orepuki (20km from Tuatapere; 68km from Invercargill). A small farming centre today, Orepuki was once a boom town. In the 1860s it attracted hundreds of gold miners who worked the beach sands, but the population swelled to around 3000 in the 1890s when an international shale-oil mining operation was developed here. The boom was short-lived, though, and the factory closed in 1902 after encountering market difficulties and problems accessing the shale. Sawmilling and, later, farming kept Orepuki going. The beach sands nearby are worth a fossick for tiny gemstones, including garnets and jaspers.

to plantation trees. Close to the town and on the banks of the river is the Tuatapere Scenic Reserve, where a stand of beech–podocarp forest provides a glimpse of how the valley must have looked before the sawmilling days. Away to the west is Fiordland National Park, a huge expanse of forest-clad ranges and valleys.

From the west side of Tuatapere a road leads south to Te Waewae Bay, Rowallanburn and Bluecliffs Beach, where the shoreline is a promenade of boulders of different colours and textures – a rockhound's delight. Look out for the fossil shells, said to be about 10 million years old, embedded in mudstone rocks. To the west is a wilderness – the Hump Range and Waitutu Forest. The spectacular Tuatapere Hump Ridge Track is a three-day tramping experience through subalpine areas and down to the south coast.

About 13km north of Tuatapere is Clifden. The limestone cliffs and caves here are an attraction, as is a large suspension bridge built in 1899. There is a small camping area at one end.

Near Clifden there is a road junction. State Highway 99 ends here, merging with State Highway 96 as it swings east towards Ohai. The Southern Scenic Route stays in the Waiau Valley, tracking north through the Blackmount district to Manapouri and Te Anau.

For an experience of a Fiordland lake, detour to Lake Hauroko from Clifden by way of the Lilburn Valley road. The lake, 31km west of Clifden, is popular among those who like tramping, camping, picnicking, fishing and boating in remote places. An easy lakeside track starts at the carpark, but be warned: the sandflies can be trying if the weather is warm, calm and cloudy. Lake Hauroko is New Zealand's deepest lake (462m).

Further north in the Blackmount area, a detour west leads to Lake Monowai and the Monowai Power Station. Borland Lodge, which has a role similar to that of Tautuku Lodge, is also on this road. Beyond the lodge the road heads for Borland Saddle, the Grebe Valley and the South Arm of Lake Manapouri – a drive recommended only for the more adventurous and well-equipped traveller. The gravel road is narrow and precipitous in places.

Sky, clouds and mountains of Fiordland reflected in the still waters of Lake Hauroko. Māori for 'moaning of the wind', Hauroko is notorious for its sudden northerly gales and can be hazardous for small boats.

WAIAU RIVER

After the Clutha, the Waiau is New Zealand's largest catchment in terms of water volumes. The Upper Waiau River links lakes Manapouri and Te Anau, but downstream of Manapouri the river is much reduced. The bulk of the water is diverted through the Manapouri power station at West Arm, New Zealand's largest hydro-electric project. The best place to experience the power of the river is from the footbridge at Rainbow Reach off the Te Anau–Manapouri road. The bridge gives easy access to the Kepler Track and some magnificent beech forest.

TE ANAU AND MANAPOURI

Lakes Te Anau and Manapouri form the main gateway to Fiordland National Park, the largest national park (1.2 million ha) in New Zealand. It occupies the remotest corner of the country. In 1986 the park became a World Heritage Area in recognition of its superb natural values – its landforms, fauna and flora. Lake Te Anau is New Zealand's second largest lake and the largest in the South Island (352 sq km). Created by glacier gouging, lakes Te Anau and Manapouri are over 400m deep, their beds well below sea level.

Journey's end, or beginning: the peaceful waterfront of Te Anau.

Te Anau is a tourist town, a jumping-off place for Milford Sound and other parts of Fiordland. It has motor camps and accommodation to suit all needs, cafés and bars, and an array of tourist services on land, water and in the air. The Department of Conservation Visitor Centre on the lakefront provides a thorough introduction to Fiordland National Park.

Manapouri, 15km south of Te Anau, is smaller – more a village than a town. It is leafy and relaxed. The lake is also smaller (142 sq km), and in this case small is beautiful. Lake Manapouri has been called New Zealand's 'loveliest lake' on account of its numerous arms, islands and sandy bays, its mountain backdrop and the way forest skirts the shoreline. Manapouri township is the starting point for visits to West Arm and Doubtful Sound.

Milford Sound is about two hours' drive north of Te Anau on a road that is tarsealed all the way.

INDEX

Bold page numbers indicate illustrations